The Publishers gratefully acknowledge assistance provided by Dr Idiculous Bluff, emeritus proponent of Bloviation at UKIP (the University of Knowledge in Practice) in preparing this book.

Publishers: Ladybird Books Ltd., Loughborough
Printed in England. If wet, Italy.

The Story of
BREXIT

by J.A. HAZELEY, N.S.F.W.
and J.P. MORRIS, O.M.G.

(Authors of 'Cheese And Onion or
 Salt And Vinegar: A Nation Divided')

A LADYBIRD BOOK FOR GROWN–UPS

Britain is a proud island. For centuries we stood alone. Now we stand alone again.

Other countries, like Croatia and Spain, need to be part of Europe, because they are clearly cowards.

But our country is special, and other countries are queueing up to get what we have to offer, whether it is the music of Sting, or any of our several mild cheeses.

This is the future.

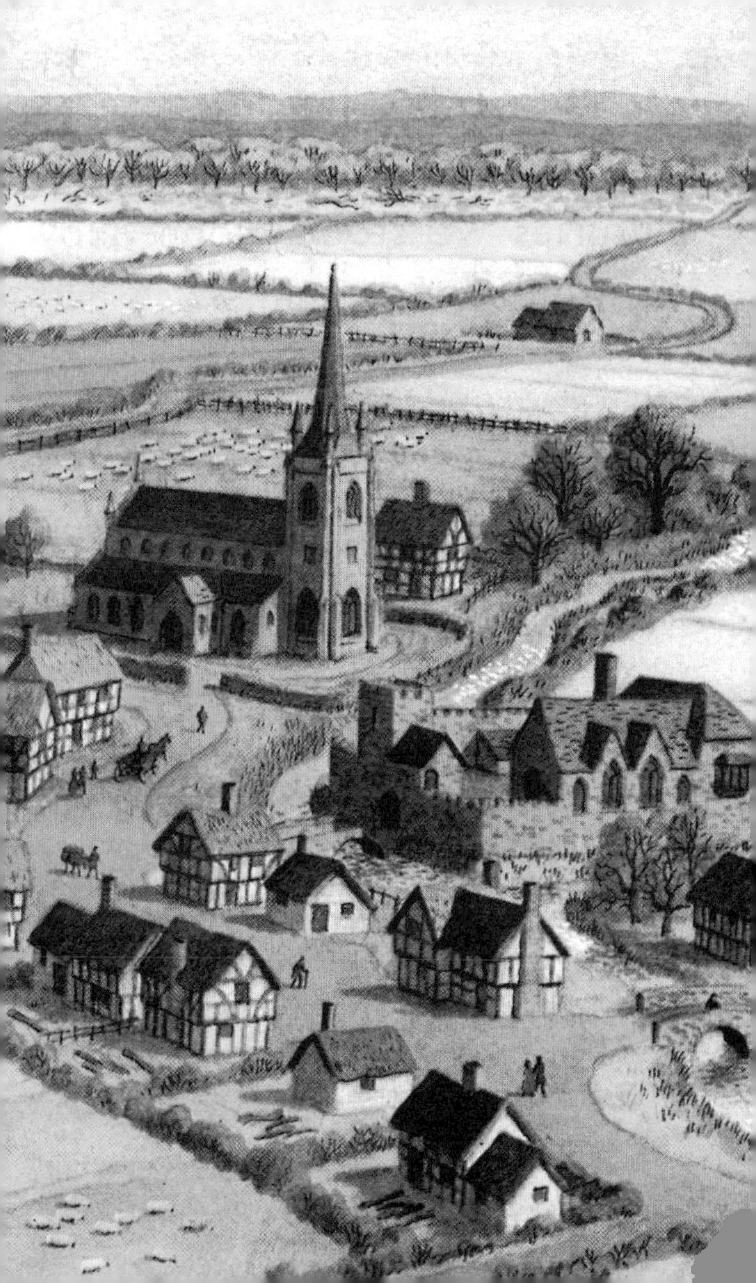

Europe is very different from Britain.

For instance, their windows open inwards rather than outwards and it is almost impossible to buy Monster Munch in Bulgaria.

No wonder we could not get along.

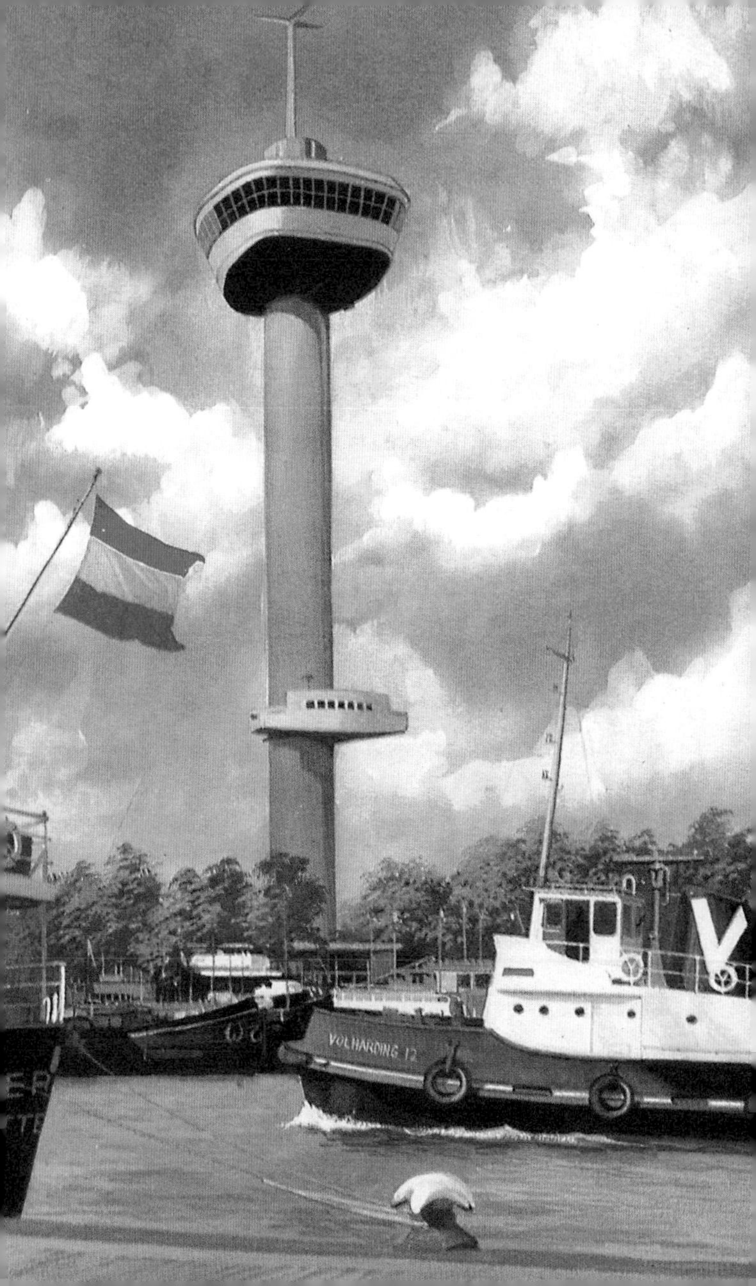
VOLHARDING 12

The British are known all over the world for keeping calm and Carry On films.

Others envy our sense of humour. We do not get "worked up". We behave with common sense and treat each other with polite good manners.

Brexit has been Britain at its best.

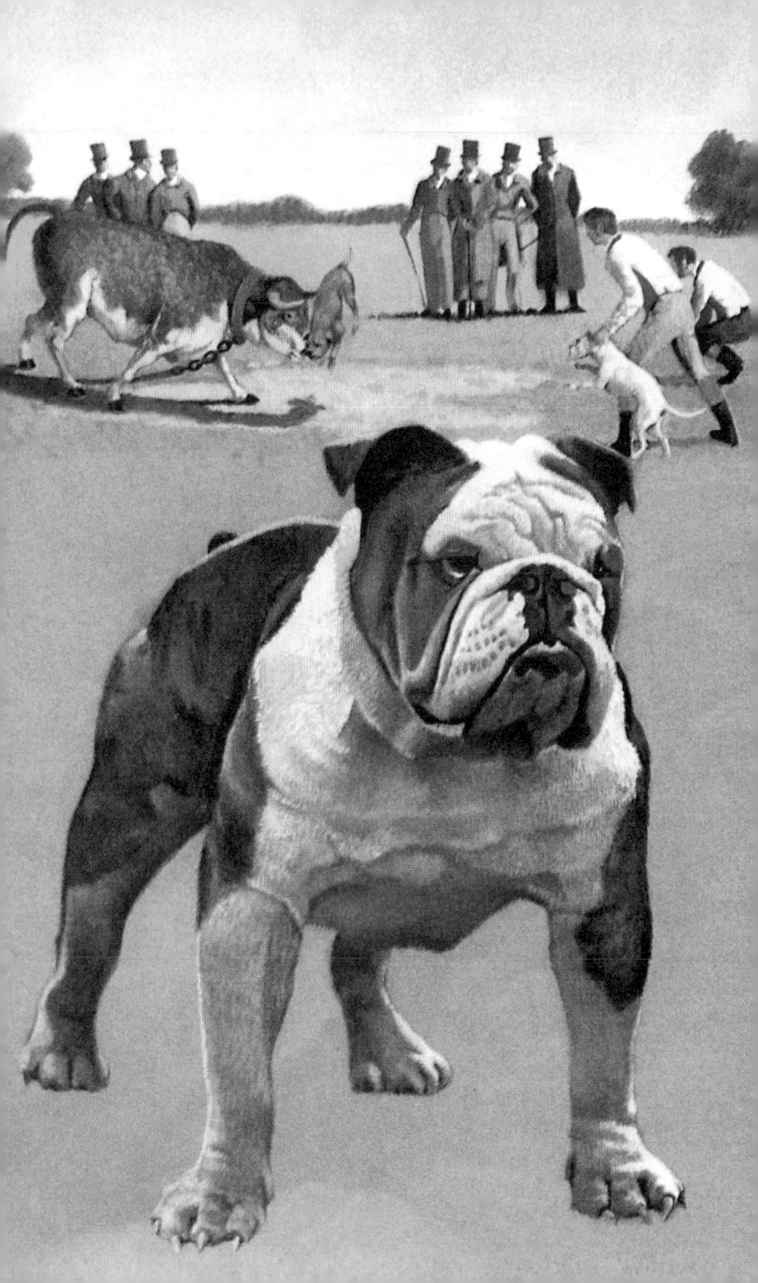

Being in the European Union is terribly complicated. Leaving it is terribly complicated too.

Luckily the choice on the ballot paper did not look very complicated at all.

It was something about freedom of bananas.

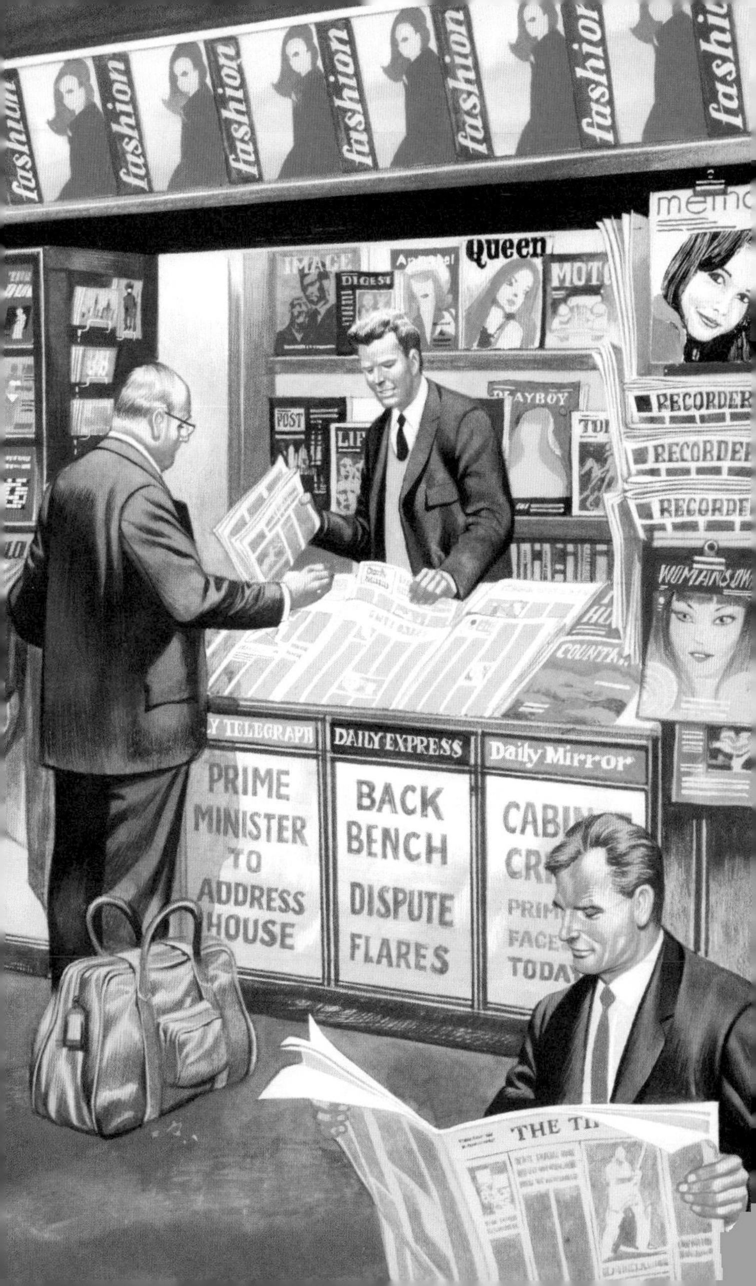
fashion
Queen
IMAGE
DIGEST
PLAYBOY
POST
RECORDER
RECORDER
Y TELEGRAPH
DAILY EXPRESS
Daily Mirror
PRIME MINISTER TO ADDRESS HOUSE
BACK BENCH DISPUTE FLARES

Like a lot of his friends, Iggy was not very interested in European federal politics. He did not know whether to vote Remain or Leave.

He was hoping there would be a third option to kick the Prime Minister out of a window.

He would have happily ticked that box.

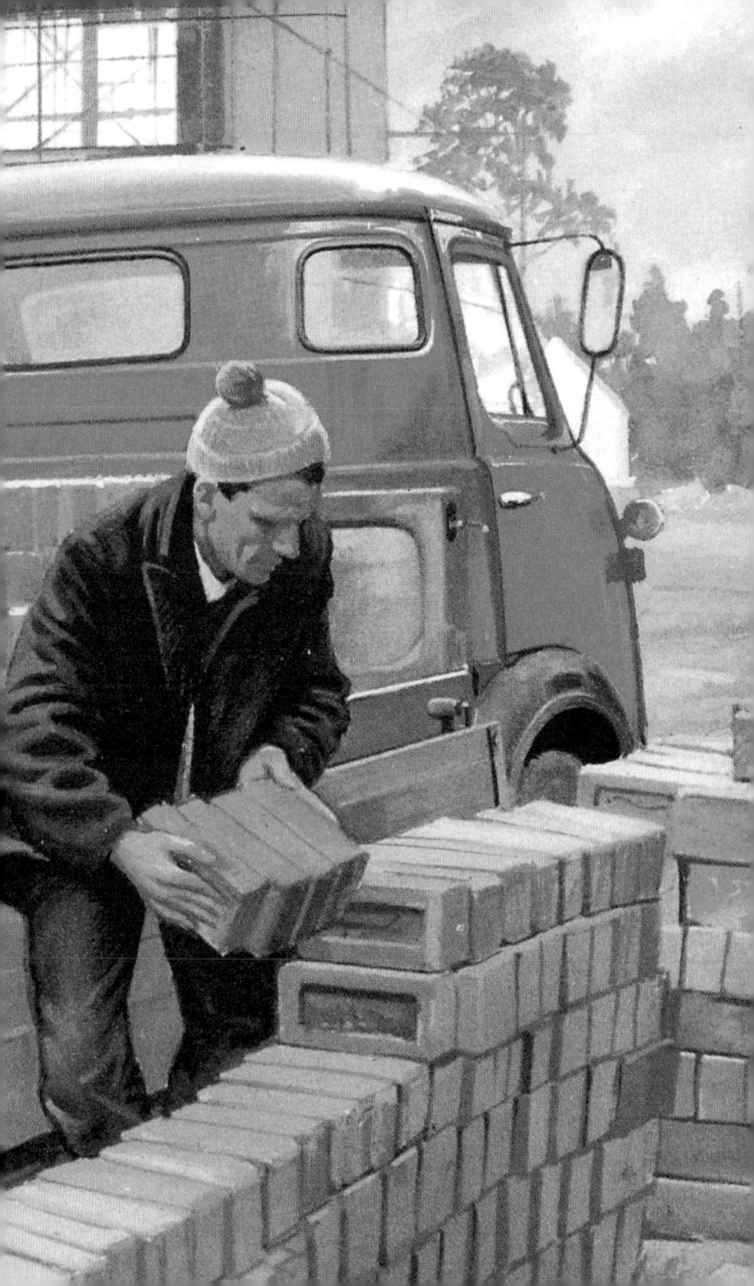

A lot of the arguments for staying in Europe were not very convincing.

Some people called it "Project Fear".

But sometimes you have to take a risk for good things to happen.

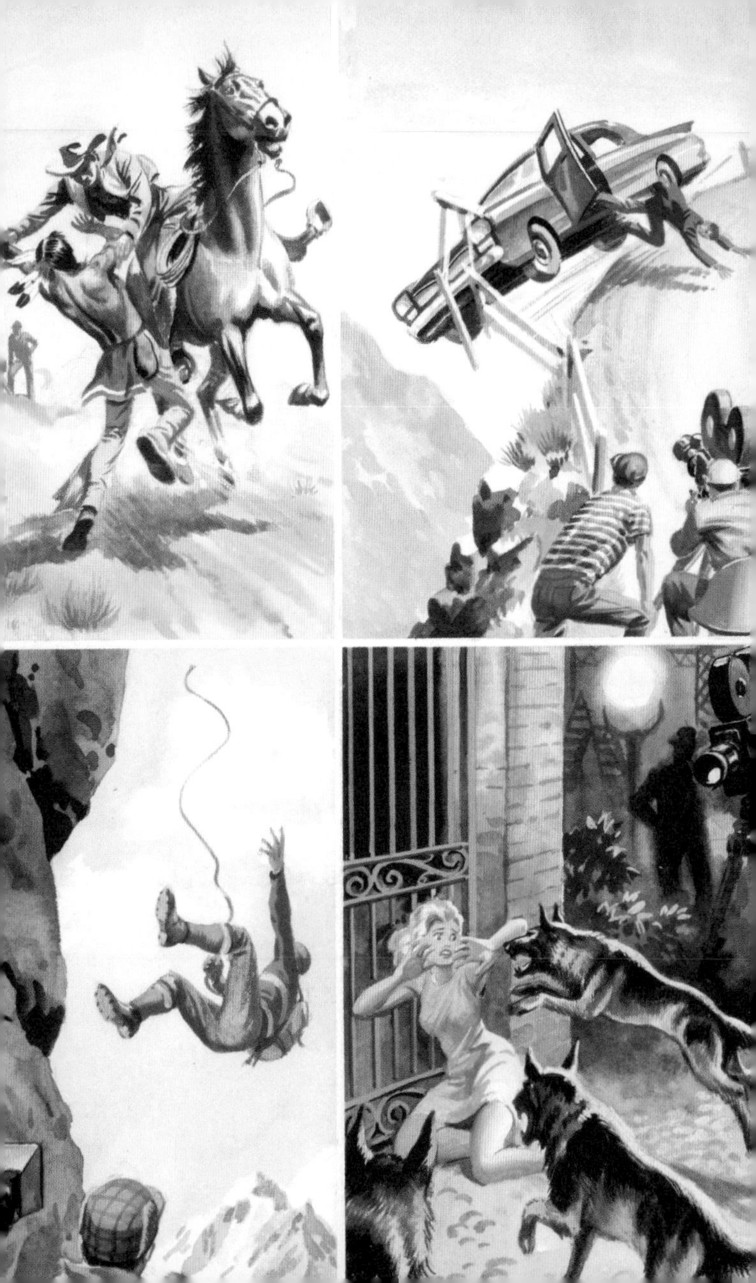

"Leaving was the will of the people," sighs Angelica's father. He voted to leave.

Angelica voted to remain, but she feels the same way. "It is the will of the people," she sighs.

They stare at the ducks. They like the ducks. Ducks are better than people.

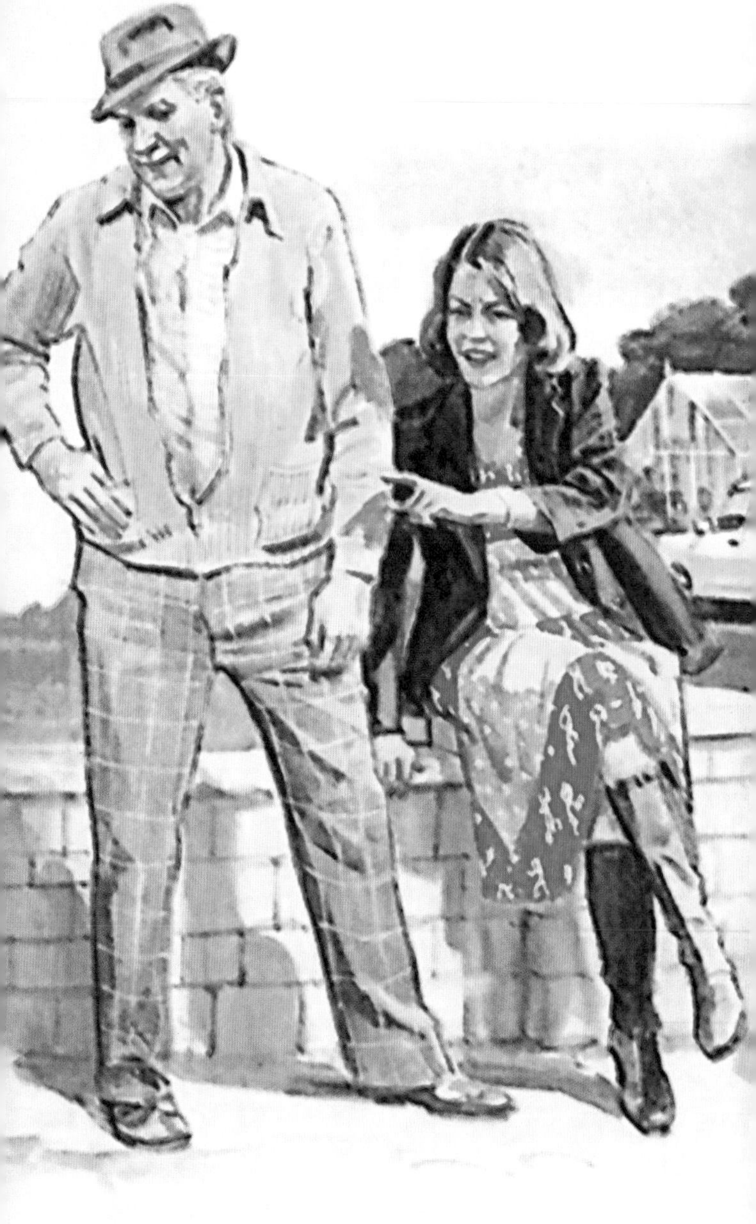

The Prime Minister organised the referendum because he was sure everybody would want things to stay exactly as they were.

But it turned out that not everybody was having as nice a time as the Prime Minister.

So the Prime Minister ran away.

It was quiet in the Prime Minister's shed.

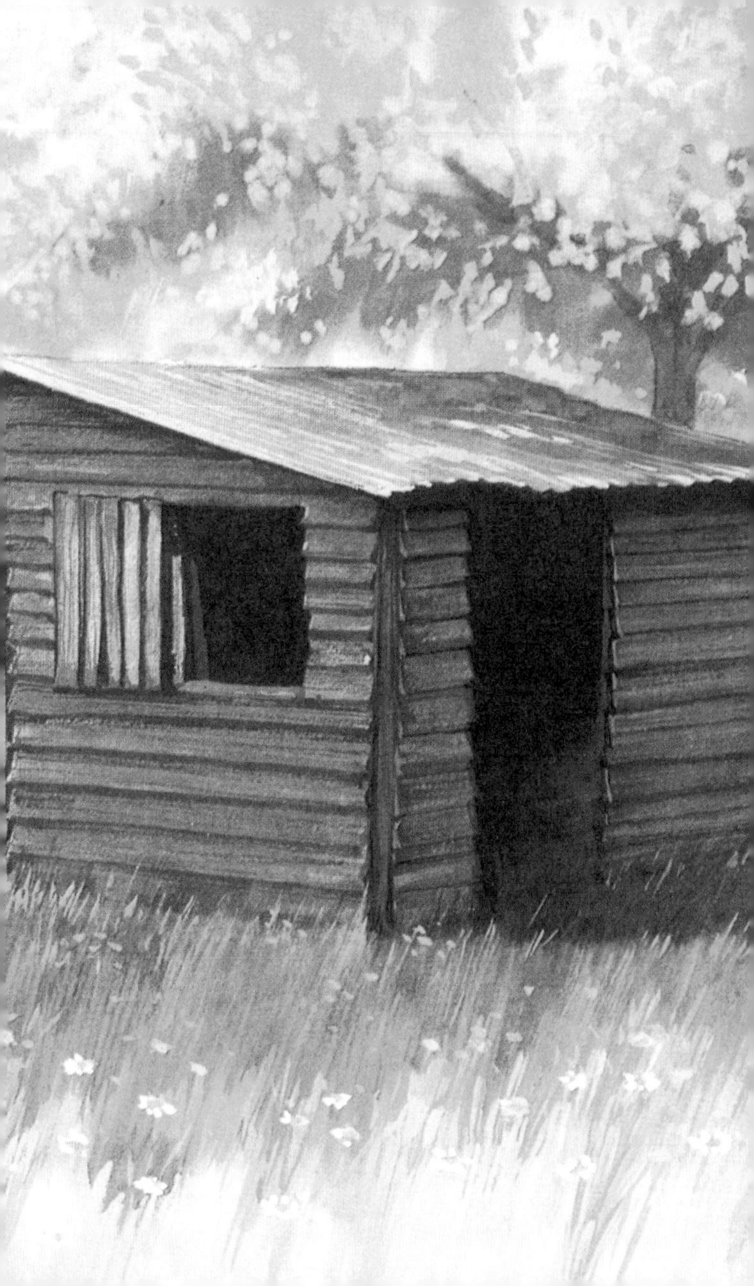

Brexit gave us lots of exciting new words, like brextremist, remoaner, bremoaner, remaybe, breprehensible, remaintenance, brexorcist, remaidstone, brex—girlfriend, remange, brextortion, remayhem and bregret.

The new words make it harder for foreigners to understand what we are saying.

In a tough, new international business world, small advantages such as this can be crucial.

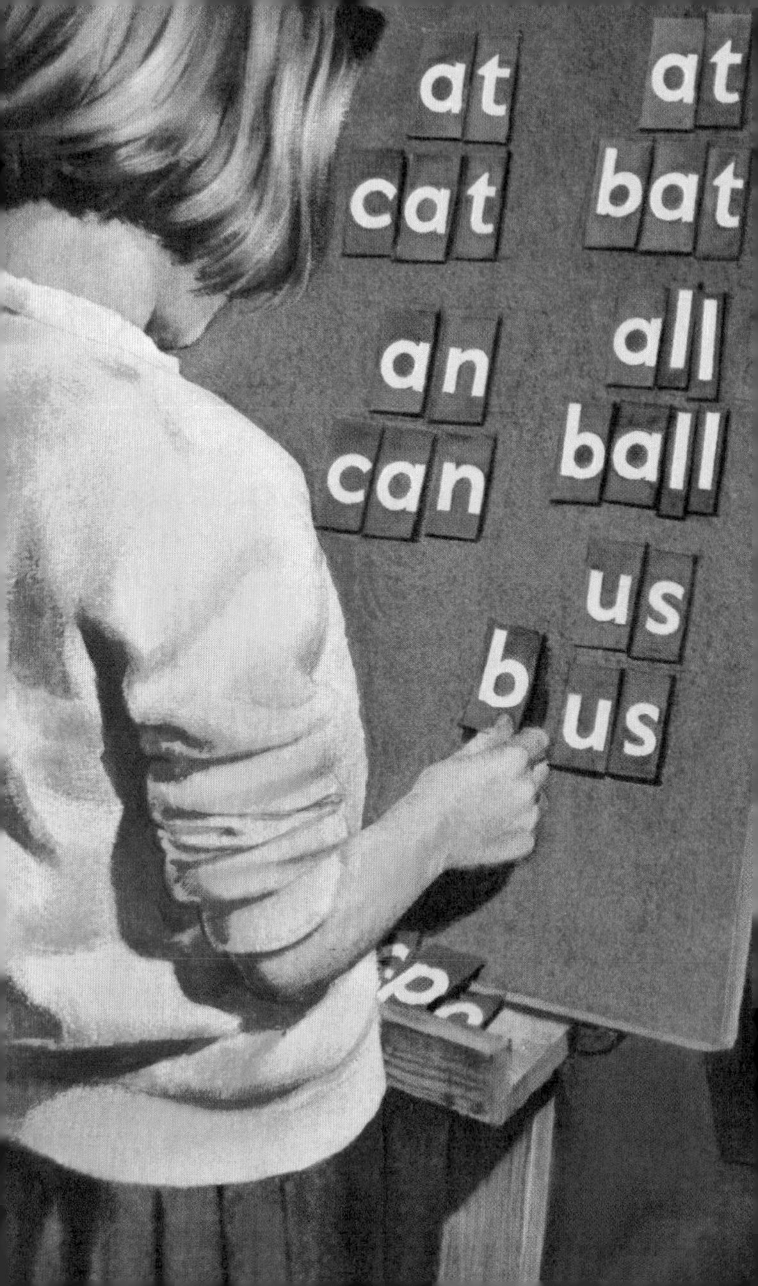
at
at
cat
bat
an
all
can
ball
us
b
us

Tess voted Remain.

She spent the morning after the referendum trying to cheer herself up by watching a film from the good old days.

She chose the film Threads.

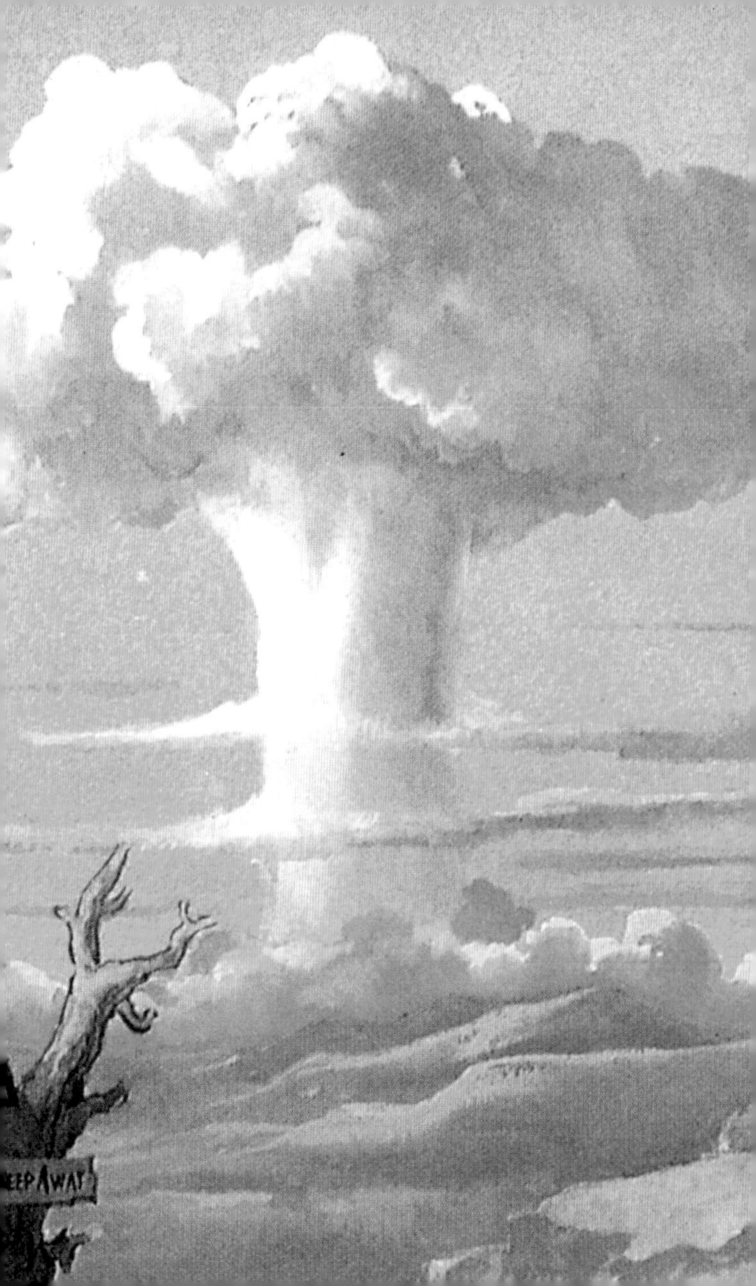
EEP AWAY

Montmorency De Douchelord Ponsonby-Fring and his friend Sir William Du Flournay were glad the public voted Leave.

Like so many land-owners, newspaper barons, hedge fund managers, firebrand back-bench M.P.s, ex-pat billionaires and Russian oligarchs, they thought it was high time the ordinary people of Britain got a chance to send a strong message to an out-of-touch elite.

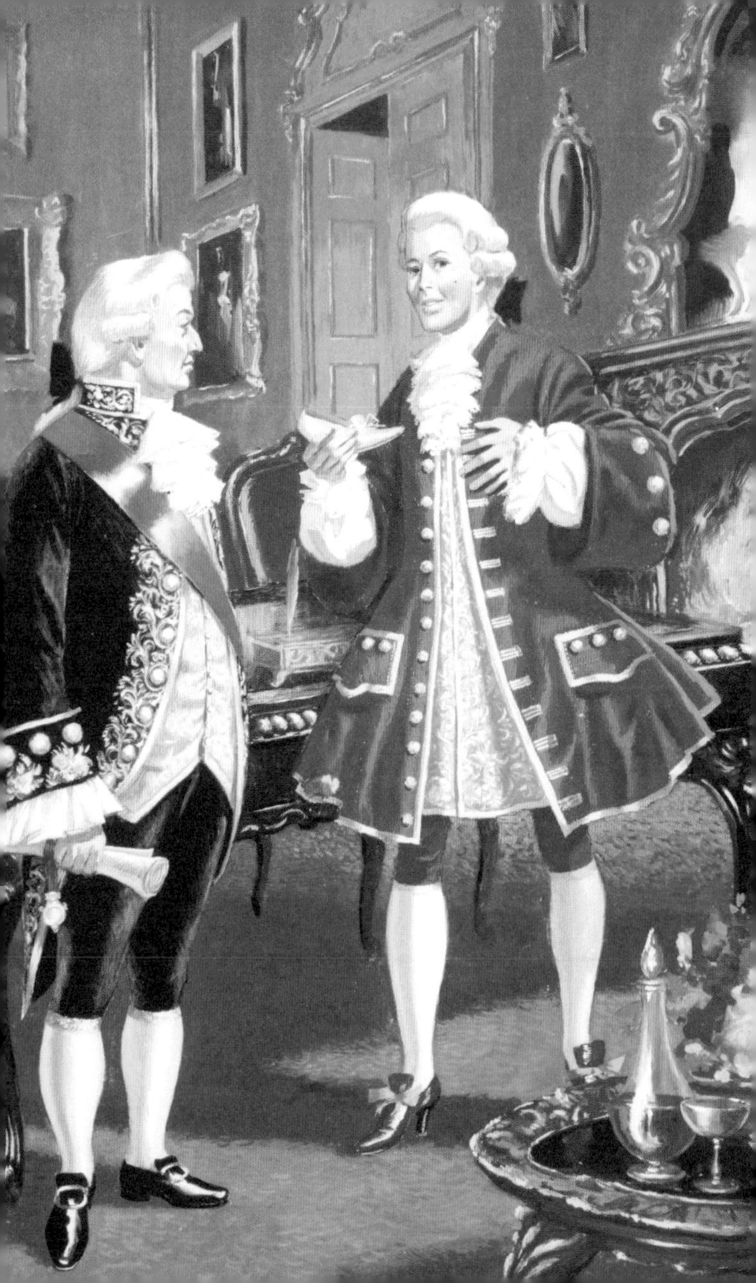

The day after the referendum, Helen woke to discover that she shared her country with millions of simply awful people she had never met who thought the exact opposite of her about most things.

Helen wonders if there could be a referendum on those people leaving instead.

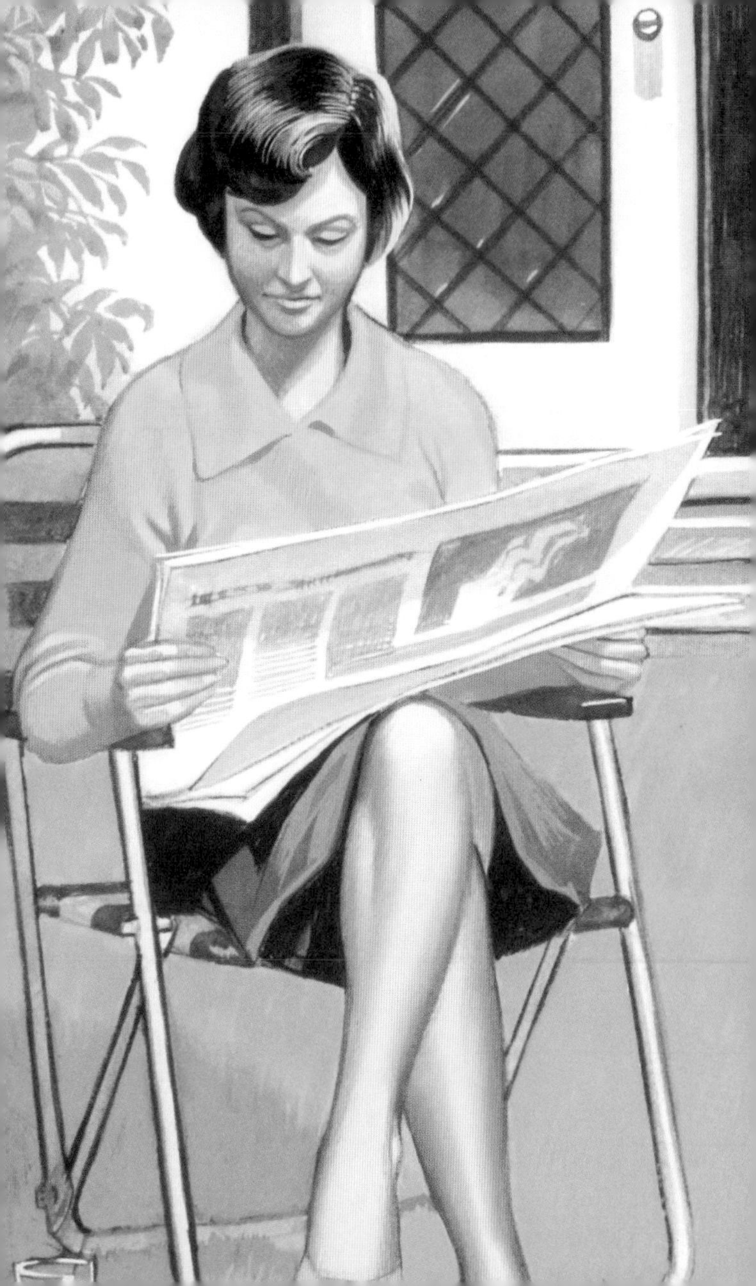

Evelyn makes lots of jam. The jam is sold all over the world. British jam is very popular.

Brexit has made Evelyn's job much easier. She can put whatever she likes in her jam, and sell it to whomever she pleases.

Without Evelyn's jam, the British economy would collapse.

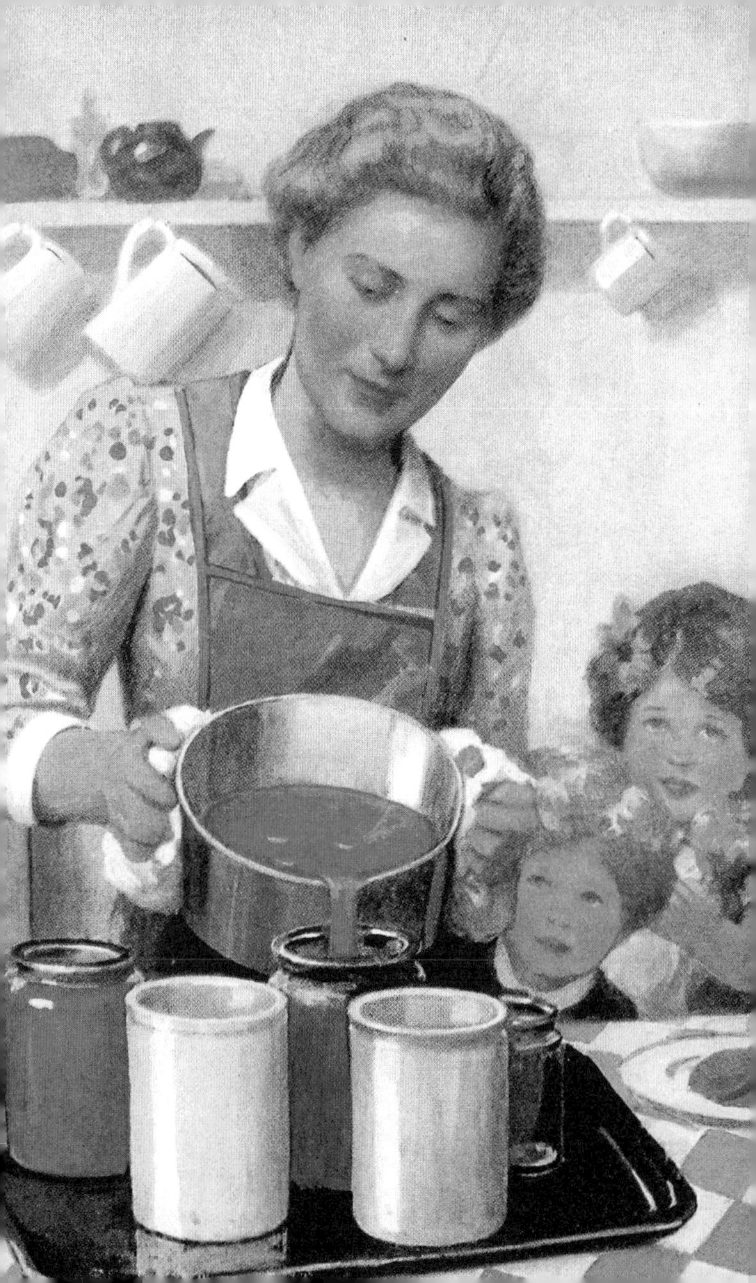

Adil and Lucy have not spent Christmas with Lucy's parents since they fell out very badly after the referendum.

They had waited many years for a good reason to spend Christmas at home.

So it wasn't all bad.

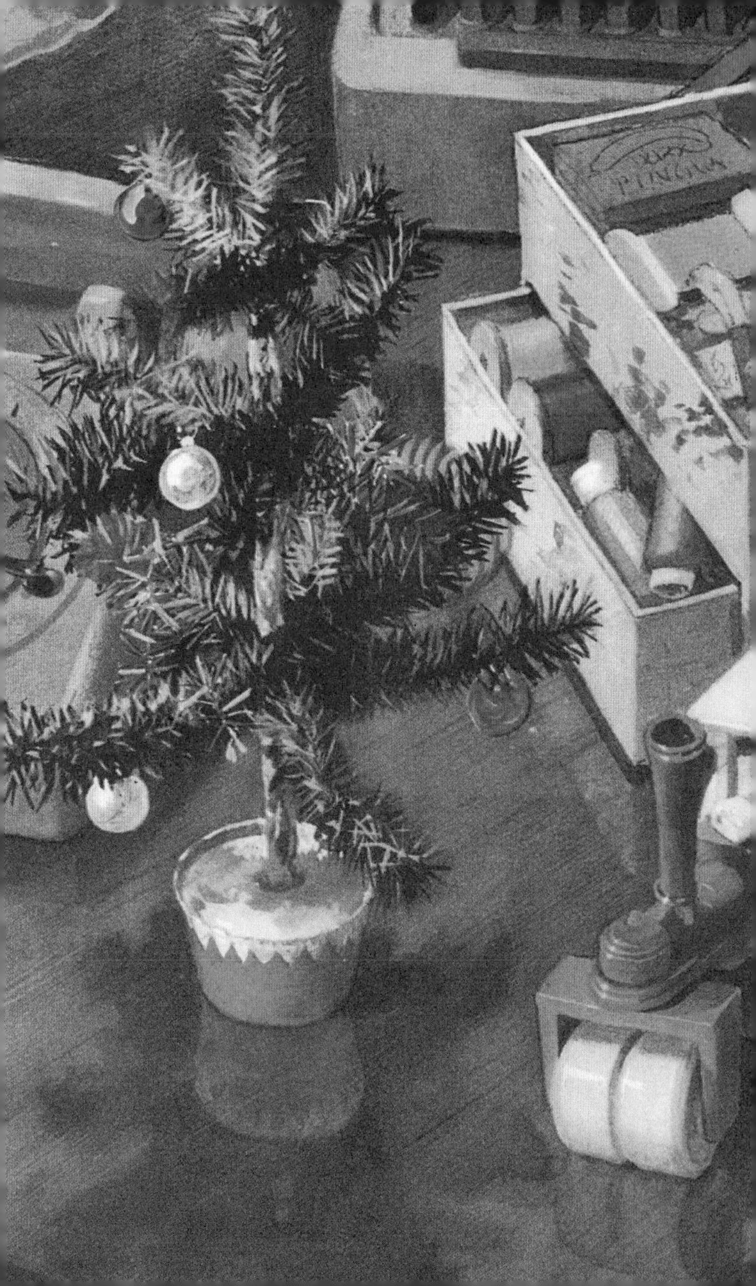

Tamara's company sends and receives information from all over the world.

While the information passes through the company's British office, it is British information and free of interfering European restrictions.

As soon as it leaves the building, it is tied up in red tape again.

But it is nice that it is free for a while.

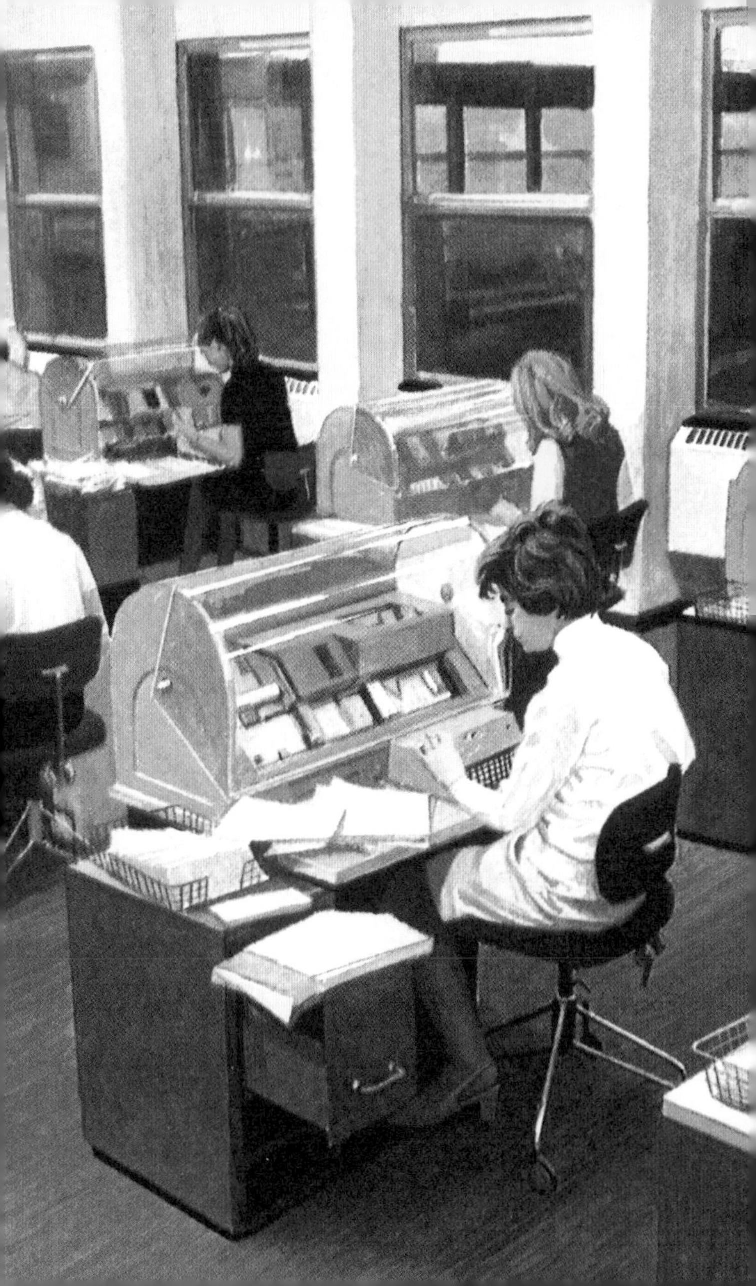

Vernon is not worried about foreign workers leaving.

"British people can mop up in hospitals and supervise veterinary conditions in abattoirs and stand in fields picking beans," he says.

Vernon will not be doing those jobs himself, of course. He is 63.

He is thinking of his nephew, Clobbo, who spends all day watching Fortnite gaming videos on Twitch.

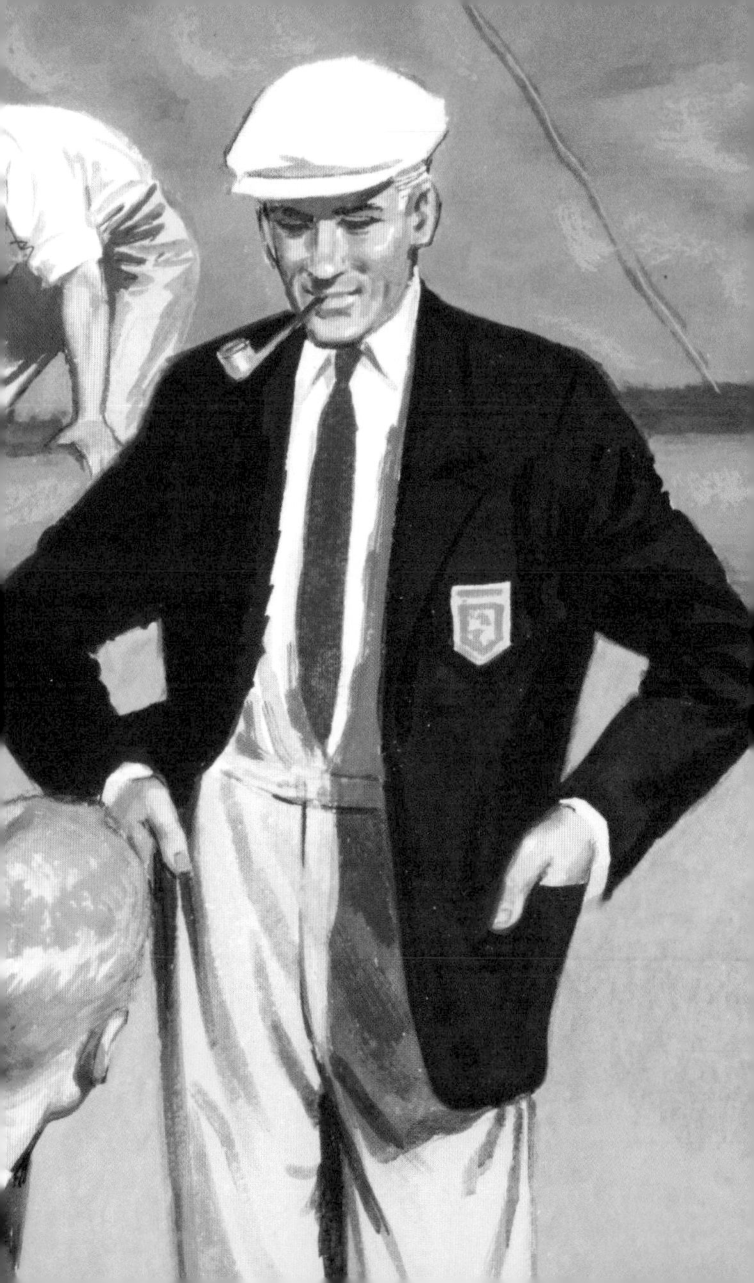

Giles heard that lots of big companies were planning to leave Britain because they thought that Brexit might be bad for business.

Giles panicked. He relocated his bucket—and—spade shop from Southend Pier to Gstaad in Switzerland.

Brexit has certainly been bad for Giles's business.

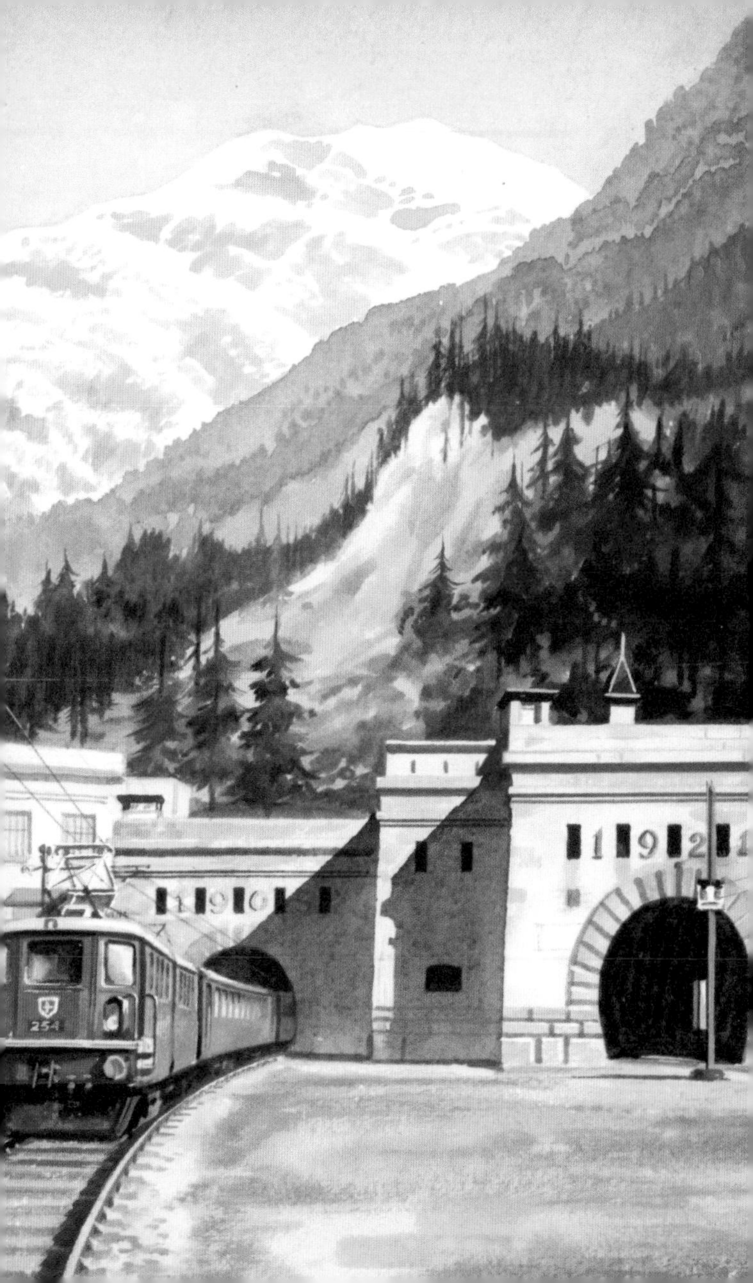
254

Diggory lives in Islington. He is a Parliamentary Private Secretary at the Department for Exiting the European Union. He has spent the last two years enacting the will of the people.

It is not the will of any people he actually knows, so he has not really done much towards it.

"Someone will work it out," he says to himself. "They usually do."

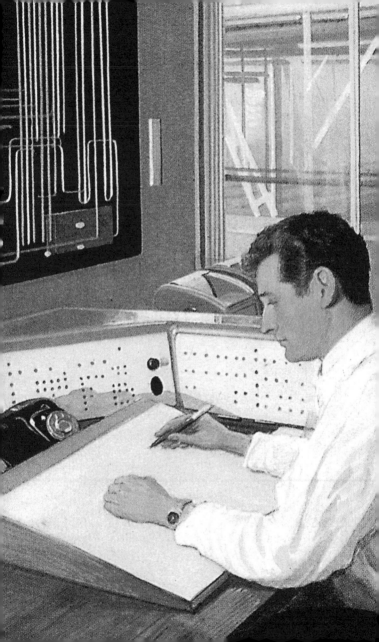

Buchanan owns a think-tank called Ideary Me which has very close links to government.

Ideary Me proposed a super-hard option called "Concrete Brexit" which would have shut down all trade with Europe and had the unemployed fighting in regional Thunder-Domes for turnips.

Buchanan also owns this real tank, so he will probably be fine, whatever.

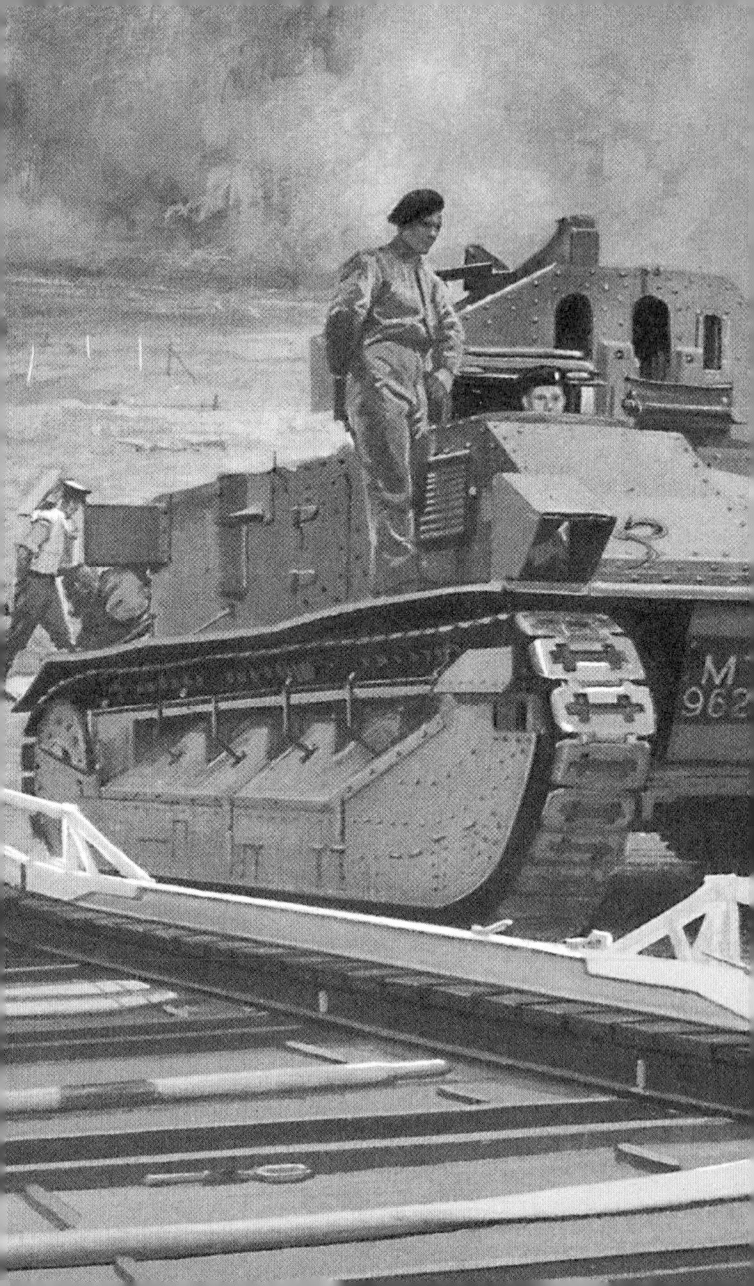

Maria applied for dual nationality because her mother is French.

Maria has never been to France.

"I don't like garlic," she says. "It smells of wet espadrilles."

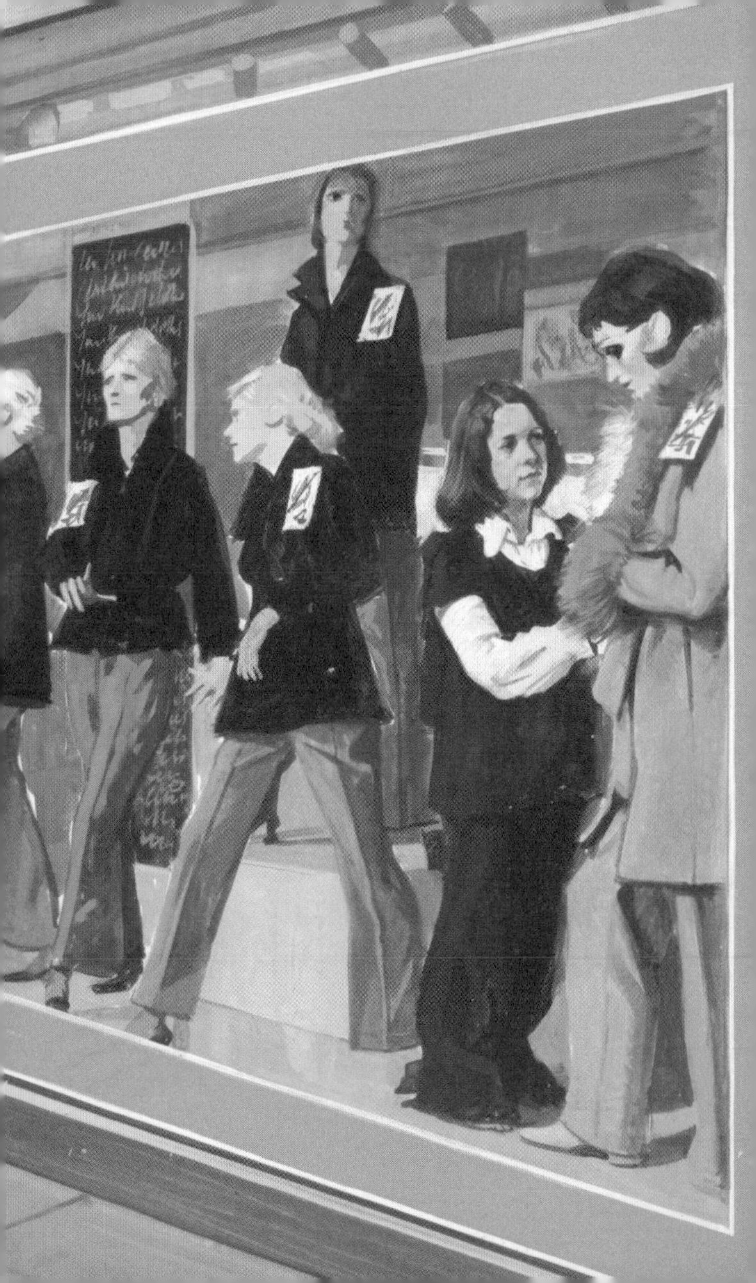

Cornwallis tells everybody that he has got his country back.

He has even started a private militia to deal with "anyone trying to enter the village who does not know the fourth verse of the National Anthem".

In the first week, he had interned thirty-eight "undesirable types", including his own plumber.

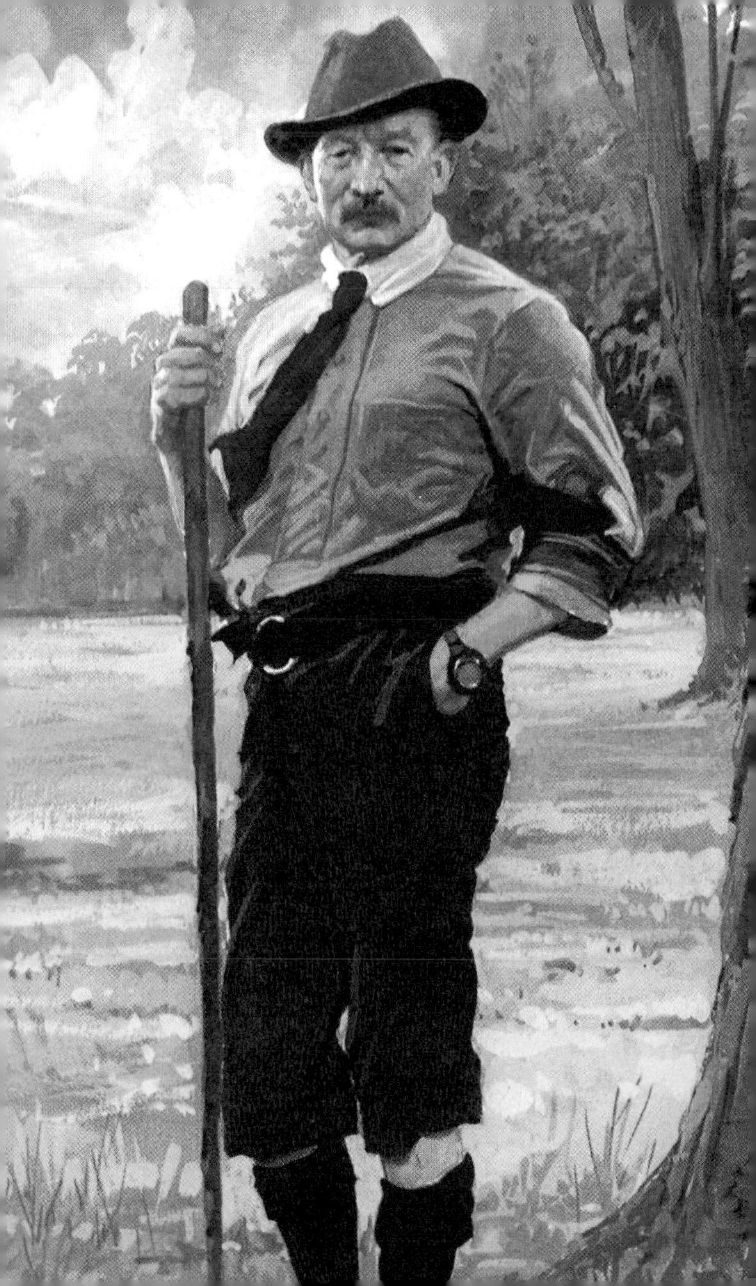

In the months leading up to the Brexit deadline, sensible people everywhere stock—piled water in case the taps went off.

A government bus drove around Britain bearing the slogan, "Only the idiots will go thirsty."

A bus is a very good way to convey important information.

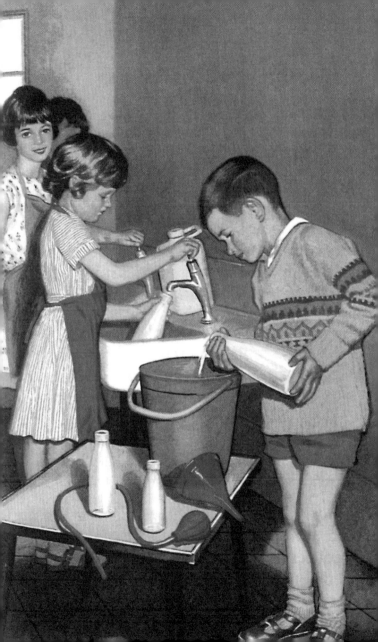

The staff of Burlington's Widgets have come on a works' outing to the theatre.

The play turns out to be a bit French.

Half of them decide to leave. They say they have plans.

They do not have plans. But they blame their friends, who remained, for ruining their night.

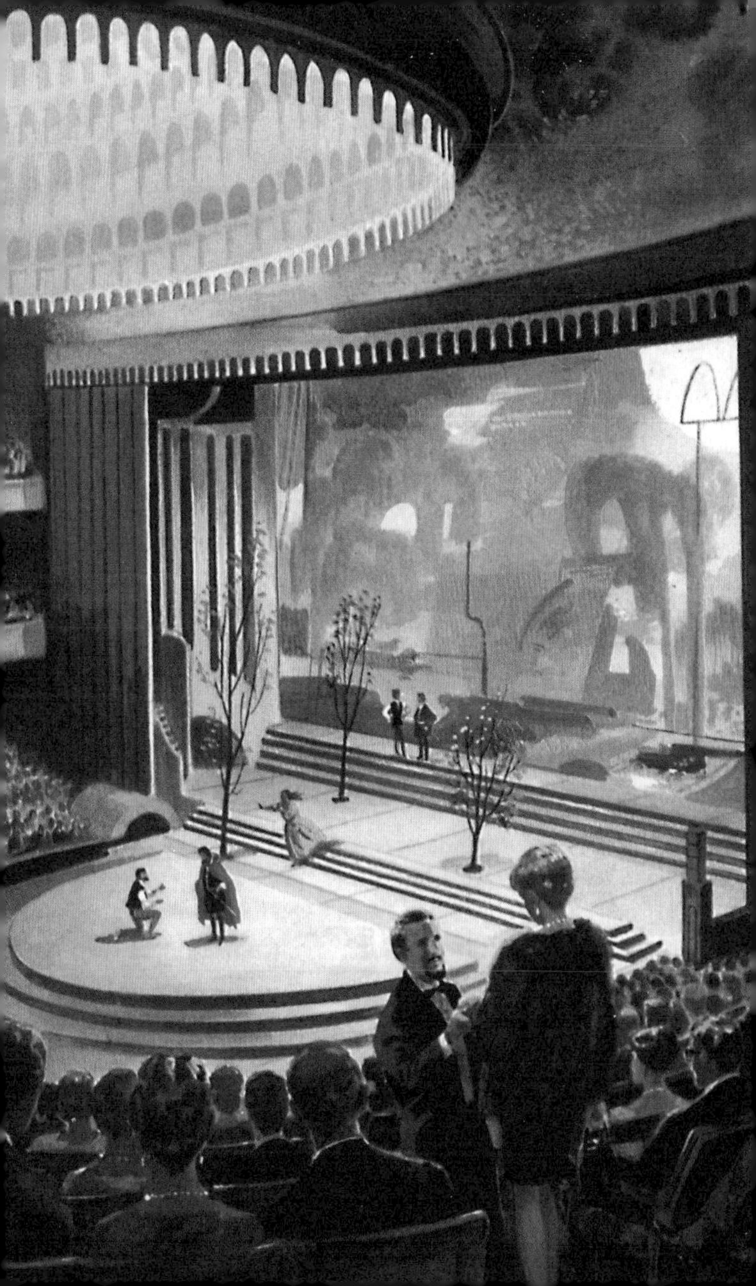

When the Nazis flew over the white cliffs of Dover, Britain fought back bravely, with nobody to help except lots of pilots from Eastern Europe, Canada, Africa, the U.S.A. and the Caribbean.

When we cracked the secrets of the Nazi Enigma code machine, we needed nothing but British ingenuity and a Nazi Enigma code machine stolen for us by some Polish spies.

We stood alone before. We can do it again — can't we?

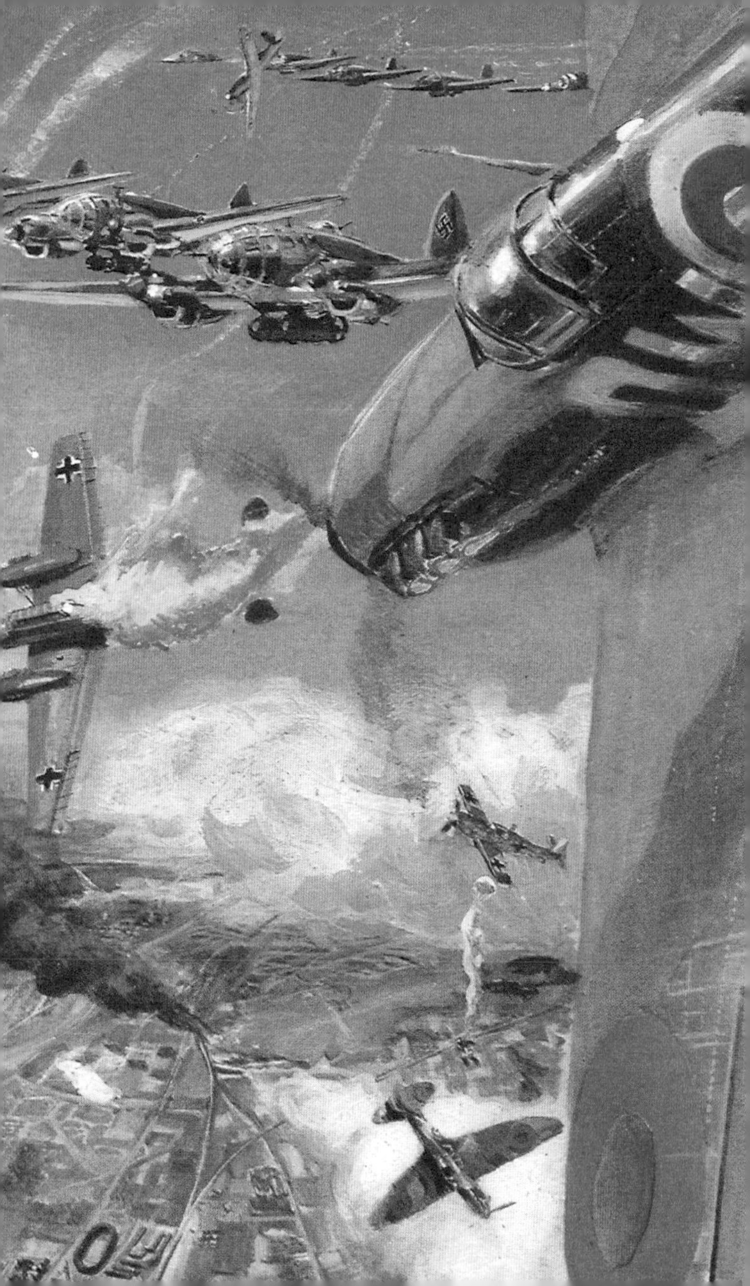

THE AUTHORS would like to record their gratitude and offer their apologies to the many Ladybird artists whose luminous work formed the glorious wallpaper of countless childhoods. Revisiting it for this book as grown-ups has been a privilege.

MICHAEL JOSEPH

UK | USA | Canada | Ireland | Australia
India | New Zealand | South Africa

Michael Joseph is part of the Penguin Random House group of companies whose addresses can be found at global.penguinrandomhouse.com

Penguin
Random House
UK

First published 2018
006

Printed in Italy by L.E.G.O. S.p.A

A CIP catalogue record for this book is available from the British Library

ISBN: 978–0–241–38656–9

www.greenpenguin.co.uk

FSC
www.fsc.org
MIX
Paper from responsible sources
FSC® C018179

Penguin Random House is committed to a sustainable future for our business, our readers and our planet. This book is made from Forest Stewardship Council® certified paper.